# The Forbidden Platform

## WOMEN IN MINISTRY

Rev. Dr. A. Louise Bonaparte

ISBN 979-8-88751-126-9 (paperback)
ISBN 979-8-88751-127-6 (digital)



Christian Faith Publishing
832 Park Avenue
Meadville, PA 16335
www.christianfaithpublishing.com

# CONTENTS

# INTRODUCTION

The title of this book seems unusual. *The Forbidden Platform* sends a message of déjà vu, does it not?

It probably provides a reminder of the very popular reference to the Garden of Eden: The Forbidden Fruit.

A woman ate the forbidden fruit first.

Like the story goes, if she had not eaten it, mankind would not be in its present predicament of sin and a lesser-than-ideal relationship with God.

However, has anyone ever stopped to think about what would have happened if Eve had not eaten the fruit?

Humans would live in a world of "kumbaya."

There would be no sorrows. No tears. No sweating to earn a living. The human experience would be peace, love, and joy.

Unfortunately, Eve ate the fruit. And now, humans have to work for their living. They also have to work for their salvation to find their way back to God.

Let us consider this predicament from a different viewpoint.

If Eve had not eaten the fruit, how would anyone be tested as to whether they truly loved God or not?

If mankind had not fallen, how would humans have been brought into a situation that requires them to innovate with their God-given intelligence in order to solve their problems? Everything would be solved for them in the Garden of Eden if they had remained there.

If mankind had not fallen, there would be nothing to strive for in God.

This could be a good thing—though we know it is a bad thing.

The reason why this perspective is being mentioned is to, perhaps, awaken our thinking to the positive side of things that are *not* considered positive by our usual society.

For instance: Eve ate the fruit—mankind sinned. Mankind has to work hard to find his way back to God. This is negative.

Or—men are active in ministry. Women want to be active in ministry. This is not traditionally acceptable. Thus, it is seen as negative too.

The topic of women being allowed into ministry is synonymous with the topic that without her, mankind would never have fallen from grace with God.

Both arguments are considered negative.

Yet, we should probably look at the positive side of it.

Why should a woman be allowed to be a minister?

While this book will not discuss Eve and the fall from the Garden of Eden, it is going to look at the other "negative" thing that women may be attempting to venture into: the topic of women in ministry.

# PART 1
## The Hall of Fame

There are multiple sayings about how women are not given as free rein in the ministry of the church as men are given.

There is also a saying, which will be mentioned here, tongue-in-check, that "What a man can do, a woman can do better!"

While this statement is not intended to offend the brothers, it is actually an opportunity for reflection.

If women are not as abundantly available in ministry as men are, perhaps, this is an opportunity for women to consider how, if they were in ministry, they could do it better.

To avoid further controversy, the real question is: What are the features of a woman having a ministry in God? What qualifies her? Or is she qualified?

The chapters of this book will build upon women that were in ministry in Biblical times. What were those features about them that caused God to recognize them as leaders?

If there is an argument today that women are not being allowed into ministry as much as men, then perhaps, the answer would be to have a study of what caused God to allow the named women in the Bible to have ministries in him. Upon understanding this, then it may answer the question of why women are not abundantly available in ministry today, and what they can do—from the perspective of the Bible—to change that story.

# CHAPTER 1

# *Deborah*

The choice of whether a man or woman leads a group will depend on God.

The prophetess in the Bible called "Deborah" proved this.

## *Deborah's backstory*

The story of Deborah does not begin from the beginning as we don't know her origins or when she actually started to lead Israel. The first time that the Bible refers to her is in chapter 4 in the book of Judges:

> *Now Deborah, a prophetess, the wife of Lappidoth, judged Israel at that time.*
>
> *She sat under the palm tree of Deborah between Ramah and Bethel in the hill country of Ephraim, and the Israelites came up to her for judgment.* (Judges 4:4–5 AMPC)

Before Deborah was first introduced in the book of Judges, it was indicated that the last judge who ruled over Israel, a man called Ehud, had died. Then came in Deborah, resolving disputes among the people while seated under a tree.

## *Despise not humble beginnings*

One can say that Deborah had humble beginnings. Her role was to resolve matters, most likely a significant number being domestic ones, while reposed under the palm tree.

The fact that people were willing to come to her to talk about their problems must have meant that she had a certain kind of wisdom, strength, or gift that enabled her to be able to pacify situations and bring peace between warring neighbors among the people of Israel.

There seems to be something about her which led to her promotion from dispute resolution between housewives to leading the commander of Israel's army into victory with the same gift of counsel that she had used for the housewives or domestic quarrels.

This may be a pointer as to why the Lord would have permitted a woman to lead the people of Israel through war times in Deborah's day. She proved herself to be trustworthy and dependable in the hands of the Lord in small matters. She helped him keep peace among the people by resolving their quarrels. It seemed a menial task. Yet, it appears, for all intents and purposes, a godly one.

After all, the type of counsel that she gave to the military general of Israel, Barak, cannot be said to be different in characteristics from the type of counsel she gave for mere domestic disputes. The military counsel was simply of a higher category.

When she was able to maintain order in the local, neighborhood arena, it seems as if she got promoted to the national, "state-wide" arena, to a place where she could now direct the state affairs of Israel.

This provides food for thought. If there is an argument against women in ministry, what if such a woman has proven herself with small beginnings so that God himself starts to send her on bigger assignments like he did with Deborah?

## *The leader in the background*

There is a saying about leaders. We have leaders at the helm of office, the people who are visibly seen by the world. Yet, in the background, there are those who are counseling them and guiding them, and they are the real leaders who probably deserve the credit, albeit unto God, if it is in the Christian environment.

Deborah was that woman who sat behind the scenes.

In Christianity or any circle, a leader is not only that individual who is visible on pulpits or in the public eye. Many true leaders are unseen, working in the background.

If that is the case, it may mean that there are more women leading ministry today than the world knows. For instance, the success of ministries may depend on the wives of the ministers. The wives support the work; they help to keep the home so that their husbands may focus on ministry. And they usually pray for God's help on the tasks.

Indeed, the focus of this book is on women who are in the limelight in ministry work. They are the women who are visibly seen, preaching on pulpits. Yet it seemed that it would be remiss not to mention the others who are in the background, leaders in their own habitats of domestic or background work, and who, without their participation in a ministry in the background, the ministerial work would not become what it was intended to be.

## When a man refuses the job

There is one more point to make about Deborah's leadership of Israel and how it is a feasible comparison to today. This last idea demonstrates an example of when the Lord may potentially decide to choose a woman as a leader.

Deborah informed the military commander, Barak, about his assignment: He needed to go to war with Sabin, the king of Canaan.

Barak pushed back on this instruction, indicating that unless Deborah went with him, he was not going.

While this speaks to Deborah's probably comforting presence and motherly nature, which would cause a military general to require her company to go to war with him, the fact still remains that Barak was, essentially, half-obeying what God wanted him to do. He was supposed to go all-in and destroy Sabin's army. God had not indicated that he should have Deborah's company with him.

Yet he wanted Deborah to go with him.

Perhaps, he was doubtful about his ability to win without the presence of the prophetess. Perhaps, he believed that if he had a prophetess like Deborah around him or close to the battlefield, he had a better chance of winning because she would be praying for him in the vicinity. Prayers travel far and do not depend on the location of a person; thus, I do not know if that argument is solid, if he considered it.

The bottom line is that Barak did not have the type of faith that would enable him to go and conquer that ministry of winning the battle for Israel.

Therefore, the Lord spoke, through Deborah: That a woman would finish Barak's work for him. A woman would be the one to kill Sabin, the work that he was being sent out to do.

Perhaps this is a good moment to pause and reflect.

The leader at the forefront, Barak, did not feel capable. God replaced the ultimate work he was supposed to do by exchanging a woman in his stead.

This may be a provocative point, and it may elicit offense in some areas of discussion. Yet, this is literally what happened. Barak was replaced because he would not do exactly as he was told.

## *The situation of replacement*

Here is an even more provocative point. Barak was replaced with a woman called Jael for the completion of the task of killing Sabin, Israel's enemy.

The question: Why did God choose a woman?

The answer: One may never know, except by making an inquiry as to why another man was not selected for the task. Was it a divine point being made from this ancient story? That in a test of wills, if a woman has the same inner grit (also known as the fire of God's will) inside of her, she is just as good to do the job as a man would?

Could the ultimate result of any ministerial job be "to get God's will done"? Or could the ultimate result be "to have a battle about reasons why a woman should not be a leader at a pulpit because it is not traditional"?

As previously mentioned, there may not be a straightforward answer.

However, as also previously mentioned, God *did* choose a woman to do a job where He would usually send a man, in the case of Deborah's story.

Could this be a recommendation that he does not mind who does the job, as long as such individual is capable of the task?

Maybe we should look at the story of another woman.

The chapters that follow will consider the lives of other women in the Bible besides Deborah.

What seems to be the Biblical perspective about their activities? This would be a good question to consider.

# CHAPTER 2
## Miriam

The Bible introduces us to Miriam when she was a young girl.

*Miriam's backstory*

The initial impression about this youngster was that she had a lot of initiative. Her story began at the birth of her little brother, the future leader of Israel. At that time, the people of Israel were living in Egypt as slaves. They had moved to that land about four hundred years earlier during a global famine. Egypt had been the only land that had food on the entire planet. It just so happened that an Israelite, Joseph, was the boss who was managing the food distribution in Egypt at that time.

Therefore, the entire people of Israel, about seventy people only at the time, a large family, moved to Egypt to be close to Joseph and the food supply.

Fast forward four hundred years to a time when Joseph and his generation had died. A new king began to rule the land of Egypt, and he was not knowledgeable about Joseph's story of four hundred years ago, and the fact that it was Joseph, the Israelite, who had saved Egypt from a famine through his ability to interpret warnings from God about natural disasters via dreams.

Moreover, at the time of the new king, the Israelites were no longer a "small" family of seventy who had originally moved to Egypt. They had grown to become a multitude of people. The exact number was not given, however, it is possible that they were as many as hundreds of thousands in Egypt by the time four hundred years rolled by.

Consider the position of the Egyptian king. Though it was a wicked point of view to have, he became quite paranoid that this large number of Israelites, who were not Egyptians, could become a threat to the land of Egypt one day. If there was war between Egypt and her enemies, the new Egyptian king believed that Israel could possibly take sides with their enemies.

He was going to proactively take care of that matter of potential future traitorship—he decided to turn the resident-visitor Israelites into slaves.

The facts were not described about how this happened of Israel's change in status or how the transition was made of a people who used to be residents in Egypt now converted into slaves.

Perhaps, one particular day, Egypt's soldiers raided the section of the land where the Israelites lived, an area called Goshen, and started to imprison them or to carry them off to work sites by force under threat of death or other harmful means. The result was that Israel knew they were—and did become—slaves. They were subject to the Egyptians that they had previously coexisted with in peace. They built cities and monuments for the Egyptians under hard slave labor.

Egypt was the superpower of that day and age. This is no wonder since they had cheap slave labor (meaning, free workers) to drive their economy!

Yet, the Israelites continued to grow in number. Egypt's king continued to grow in paranoia.

Eventually, in Exodus chapter 1, he decided that the best decision to curb the growing strength of Israel was to kill all male born sons. This was possible since Egyptian midwives were responsible for helping the Israelite women give birth:

> *The king of Egypt said to the Hebrew midwives, of whom one was named Shiprah and the other Puah, "When you act as midwives to the Hebrew women and see them on the birthstool, if*

*it is a son, you shall kill him; but if it is a daughter,
she shall live." (Exodus 1:15–16 AMPC)*

The midwives did not obey him.

In those days, Egypt worshipped objects such as the sun.

On the other hand, the Israelites believed in the God of their fathers, or God, known as Jehovah. The Bible records that the midwives were afraid of the Israelite God. This may be slightly off-topic, but the question is: What did the Egyptian midwives know about God that made them fear him, but their king did not? The possibility is that they may have had respect to Egypt's history—that it was God who had saved the Earth from a deadly famine about four hundred years earlier by warning their Egyptian king about it.

Therefore, the Egyptian midwives disobeyed Pharoah. When asked why, their excuse was that the Israelite women were very strong. They had already given birth in all cases before the midwives arrived to help them—they explained to the king!

The midwives got tangible rewards for their fear of killing the babies or offending the God of Israel. The Bible records that God blessed their homes.

(Blessing means to be "happy," "to be enlarged." Therefore, God gave the midwives peaceful, happy homes and material things to increase their station in life.)

Pharoah decided on another tactic to subdue Israel's population growth. Since the midwives claimed they could not intercept and kill the Israelite male sons, he decided he would send his soldiers to do it.

The soldiers were to raid the Israelite dwelling area from time to time it seems. Any male child born would be killed.

The story of Miriam is not forgotten in all these. How did she come into the picture?

## *The birth of Moses*

There was an Israelite man/slave called Amram who got married. He married a girl called Jochebed. They had two children: Aaron and Miriam.

At the time they were about to have a third child, Pharoah's wicked decree—to kill male Israelite babies—came into existence. The story goes like this:

> *The woman (Jochebed) became pregnant and bore a son; and when she saw that he was [exceedingly] beautiful, she hid him three months.*
>
> *And when she could no longer hide him, she took for him an ark or basket made of bulrushes or papyrus [making it watertight by] daubing it with bitumen and pitch. Then she put the child in it and laid it among the rushes by the brink of the river [Nile].*
>
> *And his sister [Miriam] stood some distance away to* [a]*learn what would be done to him.* (Exodus 2:2–4 AMPC)

This is where Miriam's story begins.

## Miriam, her brother's keeper

The helpless baby, Moses, was left floating on the river Nile. As babies are known to do, of course, he began to cry. He must have been hungry.

Pharoah's daughter was taking a bath close by. She heard the child. She asked her servants to go fetch him. She decided to keep the baby. This was where Miriam sprang into action.

It is not clear whether her mother and father had put her up to it to go and watch what may happen to her little brother. It is likely that they did. Whether or not the instructions were from them, this may be the beginning of Miriam's call to be her brother's keeper.

She was not intimidated about the prospect of going to speak with Egyptian royalty. Consider a girl's position, a *girl-slave*, in comparison to a nation's princess. How much boldness would it have taken for her to come out of hiding and go speak to the princess by saying: "Shall I find a wet nurse to feed the baby for you?"

A practice in those days was that women (particularly the wealthy ones) could hire nannies who could breastfeed so that the nanny took care of feeding the baby while its wealthy mother did not have to. It would not have been an unusual question when Miriam went up to the princess to ask it.

The princess agreed. Miriam went to fetch her own mother, who had, of course, only recently given birth and therefore, could breastfeed the child—and Moses got to be fed by his own mother till he was old enough to be taken to the palace to live with the princess.

## *Miriam's role in Moses' survival*

It seems that when a person plays a role in preserving or looking after the interests of God's servants, that person may receive an honorary position in God's offices. It would not matter whether the person was male or female.

This is only a fleeting suspicion. However, the fact that Miriam had been able to speak to a princess boldly may recommend that she could have had a hand in, physically steering Moses' little basket in the direction of where the princess was having a bath because she was brazen enough to do so.

*The right destinies do not just happen by chance—someone has to take action.* Moses' destiny to stay alive and, eventually, be the Israelite leader did not just happen by chance. A series of actions had to take place—and Miriam was one of those actors who played a part in it.

For this reason, this chapter will make a bold statement (no pun intended). Miriam *may* have been noticed by God as a future *female* leader because of her boldness. It seems that the Lord takes note of bold people. There are several accounts in the Bible in which the Lord approves of boldness or speaks of it.

There were many capable men in Israel in Miriam's day who could have been selected to be the companions of Moses, the Israelite leader. Miriam was picked. There may be arguments that she was chosen because she was his sister. Perhaps, nepotism was at play?

However, this would be a great fallacy. It is obvious throughout Scripture that God does not play nepotism.

He passed over Jesus's biological brothers when allotting discipleships. A passage in Scripture reads:

> *Someone said to Him (Jesus), Listen! Your mother and Your brothers are standing outside, seeking to speak to You.*
>
> *But He replied to the man who told Him, who is My mother, and who are My brothers?*
>
> *And stretching out His hand toward [not only the twelve disciples but all] [v]His adherents, He said, Here are My mother and My brothers. (Matthew 12:47–49 AMPC)*

Jesus's biological family came to see him. He did not give them preferential treatment.

As well, God passed over the firstborn sons of Jesse, the most capable looking men, when choosing a king for Israel.

> *When they had come, he (Samuel) looked on Eliab [the eldest son] and said, Surely the Lord's anointed is before Him.*
>
> *But the Lord said to Samuel, Look not on his appearance or at the height of his stature, for I have rejected him. For the Lord sees not as man sees; for man looks on the outward appearance, but the Lord looks on the heart. (1 Samuel 16: 6–7 AMPC)*

There are other examples throughout Scripture to show that God does not choose people based on popular opinion. He looks at human beings' hearts to determine who is capable of the task.

As one progresses in reading through the book of Exodus in the Bible, it becomes apparent that Miriam became a prophetess. Prophets or prophetesses (female) are inspired speakers who are said to be able to see into the future. It is a position that God has been known to give to people that he approves for his special offices.

Therefore, Miriam was approved by God as she was given an office by him. This brings us *back* to the question: Why?

If there were men in Israel who were capable of being close companions to Moses as Miriam was, why did God select her and not one of the men?

This may go to show that from the period of the Old Testament, God has been selecting women for offices in his kingdom when he finds them *capable* of the task.

The test for gaining positions in God is, therefore, not gender but capability.

In the next chapter, another female leader would be considered to test this point about the capability requirement that qualifies women for offices in the church.

# CHAPTER 3
# Queen Esther

Esther became a queen by divine opportunity.

The king of Persia, King Ahasuerus, had a wife, Queen Vashti. However, some historical opinions suggest that Vashti may have been an ancient day "feminist."

## Esther's backstory

The king was holding a big party. He ordered that Vashti should come to his court to display herself before his nobles and guests. The accounts from historical views mentioned in the reference section of this book indicate that Vashti was a beautiful woman, and the king wanted to show her off. She refused. It may have been an act of defiance to demonstrate that she would not be a showpiece at the whim of her husband.

In looking at Biblical accounts, the only people that had been able to get away with defiance toward rulers of ancient times were those who were being defiant because God Himself was backing them up.

## *Shedrach, Meshach, and Abednego*

King Nebuchadnezzar ordered the people of his land to bow down to his golden image. Three Israelites refused:

> *Shadrach, Meshach, and Abednego answered the king, O Nebuchadnezzar, it is not necessary for us to answer you on this point.*
>
> *If our God Whom we serve is able to deliver us from the burning fiery furnace, He will deliver us out of your hand, O king.*
>
> *But if not, let it be known to you, O king, that we will not serve your gods or worship the golden image which you have set up! (Daniel 3:16–18 AMPC)*

They were thrown into a fiery furnace. They had to be taken out of the fire because it did not burn them as the Lord did not permit it.

## *Peter:*

Peter was an apostle of Jesus, going about cities, preaching the Gospel of Jesus Christ. His preaching was in defiance to the orders of rulers of the day, who demanded that he and other disciples should stop. Herod, the king, had him arrested and the following happened:

> *So, Peter was kept in prison, but fervent prayer for him was persistently made to God by the church (assembly).*
>
> *The very night before Herod was about to bring him forth, Peter was sleeping between two soldiers, fastened with two chains, and sentries before the door were guarding the prison.*
>
> *And suddenly an angel of the Lord appeared [standing beside him], and a light shone in the place*

*where he was. And the angel gently smote Peter on the side and awakened him, saying, Get up quickly! And the chains fell off his hands. (Acts 12:5–7 AMPC)*

Peter walked out of prison because the Lord did not permit his remaining there.

There are other examples that can be provided about people in Biblical history who were defiant to ungodly decrees of the leaders of their day—those who were doing it because of their stand and faith in God generally got God's help.

For those who were being defiant to leaders of the day out of their pride and personal defiance, they got disgraced.

This is the point where the story of Esther will be introduced.

## Esther—queen of the Persians

As previously mentioned, Queen Vashti was defiant to her husband, the king. She refused to come out to the party when he instructed it (Esther 1:12).

The result: She was stripped of her royal title, and he divorced her. It was a sad price to pay for her taking an unwise stand. Taking stands require adequate support and prudent considerations.

Esther was chosen as queen after a vigorous selection process. There were many other women who were gathered around the provinces which King Ahasuerus ruled over. Yet, Esther came out as the preferred candidate to be the new queen.

Of course, her real position as queen was intended to be one of a servant, an underling of the king. She served the king just like his other subjects. She was required to obey his rules.

There was a particular rule in the court that unless the king summoned a person to him in his royal courtroom, their showing up without invitation would result in their death.

A situation arose that required Esther to go and see the king in his courts without invitation.

Esther was Israelite by nationality. The king did not know this and neither did most or all his nobles. In those days, there was a noble man in the king's court called Haman, who had a dislike for one particular Israelite in the kingdom—the Israelite called Mordecai.

Mordecai also happened to be Esther's uncle, but it seems their relationship was not widely known.

Haman, the noble man, was a proud man. He loved it when people bowed to him as he walked through public places. As it is the custom of Jews or Israelites who fear God, they do not bow to men or images.

Therefore, Mordecai would not bow to Haman anytime the nobleman walked by in public places.

Haman took note of this. After all, the Jew would have stood out as a sore thumb among the common people who were obediently bowing down to Haman. This gesture alone (Mordecai's act that was in respect of God), was what bred the hatred in Haman's heart that made him decide that he wanted Mordecai—and anyone associated with him—to die!

Haman devised a plan to eliminate Mordecai for good. He decided to make the king write up a decree. As an adviser to the king, Haman's suggestion to the king was intended to be "advice" that would protect the king's interests. He told the king:

> *There are a certain people scattered abroad and dispersed among the peoples in all the provinces of your kingdom; their laws are different from every other people, neither do they keep the king's laws. Therefore, it is not for the king's profit to tolerate them.*
>
> *If it pleases the king, let it be decreed that they be destroyed, and I will pay 10,000 talents of silver into the hands of those who have charge of the king's business, that it may be brought into the king's treasuries. (Esther 3:8–9)*

Haman recommended destruction of the Jewish people. Of course, since the king trusted him as an adviser, he agreed to it.

## Giving her life

A woman who is truly meant for ministry is one who can give her life for people—literally.

This is the core of what Esther did. She knew there was a law in the land—no one appears before the king unless summoned. She was willing to take the risk, albeit, after seeking God for help and support. She did indicate though that even if God did not show up to help her, *"Then I will go to the king, though it is against the law; and if I perish, I perish"* (Esther 4:16 AMPC).

This was the true mark of a leader. A woman who was ready to lead and ready to die for people for a just or right cause, not foolishly, of course.

## The wisdom and discernment of Esther

Before Esther heard of the decree that had been released to kill the Jews, being a Queen in her tall castle, she was quite oblivious to the events going on outside the palace with her people. Mordecai, her uncle, sent a message to her.

She was a wise woman. She may have recalled the defiance of her predecessor toward the king, Queen Vashti. A person, no matter what position they think they have, would be foolish in trying to rebel against authorities, especially if they had no stronger authority that was backing them up.

As previously mentioned, the rule of the royal courts was that no one should show up to see the king except when they were summoned. If they showed up without a summons, they would be put to death. Esther had not been summoned to the royal court in a while. Therefore, if she defiantly went there just because she was queen, she stood the chance of getting killed.

She fasted for three days. She asked Mordecai to inform the nation of Israel living in that land to fast for her as well. She was going to show up—defiantly—to the king's court, but she was going to do it by seeking God's support.

There are instances in the Bible where God has frowned at disobedience to authority. This was exactly what Esther was doing—she was just about to disobey the authority of her husband.

However, a leader is recognized by the decisions they are able to make in the midst of "gray areas." The gray area here was that Esther was going to disobey the king, but it was for a good cause—to ask him to spare the lives of the Israelites.

Yet, was this not what Vashti had done that made her lose her crown? She had disobeyed the king but for a "good" cause—to protect women's rights.

The story of Esther is proof that a good cause is defendable only when one is wise to back it up with an authority that is greater than the institution which is opposing it.

*Esther proves that she was a female leader by reason of wisdom and discernment.*

She fasted and prayed to the Lord that he would help her as she took the necessary step to go and speak to the king about her people and keeping them alive. She sought the support of a higher authority than the king.

Then, she went to the king's court, uninvited. A taboo in the land.

Lo and behold—he was so happy to see her. He asked her what she wanted, and he would give it, even half of his kingdom!

Esther was able to ask him to come to a banquet that she would throw for him and for his nobleman, Haman.

The king obeyed like an obedient subject! She invited him and Haman to two banquets. At the second banquet, she reported Haman's plot to the king while Haman was present. She pointed him out as a conspirator who was trying to kill an entire nation of innocent people.

She had prayed. She had fasted. She was not doing this out of her pride or personal defiance.

The king listened to her. He had Haman and his family hung.

## *When the office is not due to personal defiance*

The phrase "personal defiance" has been repeated over and over in this chapter. It was first mentioned with Vashti. She had a point to prove, and therefore, she set out to prove it. God was not with her, only her convictions and her pride that she deserved to be treated better. She got disgraced.

Esther, on the other hand, took a different approach. Every office and every step that she took throughout the book of Esther was by divine help.

She did not step into the office of "hero of the people of Israel" by thinking: *I am a queen. It is my right as a child of God. It does not matter whether I am female. I ought to be allowed into this position to save Israel from their enemies!*

She did not think in such a manner. Instead, she waited on the Lord. Her position as queen was not good enough to give her a position in God's offices. He had to hand it to her himself. And it is apparent that he did, judging by the huge favor that Esther found in her husband's sight upon entering his court.

The role of a female leader is not one that anybody can step into just because they think the opportunity is right.

The story of Esther shows that as a queen, meaning a highly titled person, if she had not received God's support, she stood the chance of getting killed if she had stepped into a godly role, such as one which saved Israel from death if God was not supporting it.

Male leaders are appointed more easily in churches. In some cases, some should probably not be in the offices they occupy because they are not approved by God himself.

As for female leaders, because the question of their being leaders in the church is not as easily resolved as for males, it is actually a good place to be. It means that she has an example from Esther to follow. She needs to pray and fast and not step into offices that God did not tell her to take.

It could mean death to take a God-role that is not supported by God: Maybe not physically, as with Esther's situation but in other figurative ways.

To conclude, God allowed Esther into this leadership position to face the king because she had the wisdom to be led by him into it. She did not take it upon herself out of pride.

Therefore, a female leader on matters of work for God is not frowned upon by the Lord according to this story.

She simply needs to have the wisdom to know how to involve God in her heart's desire to lead.

He may approve, and He may not. The office of a female leader in the church or to lead God's people is not automatic as is obvious from Esther's case.

# CHAPTER 4
## *Rebecca*

Rebecca's story is a favorite with anyone who likes stories about destiny.

The Bible introduces her when she was very young. She may have been a teenager, or at least, a very young adult. The first time that we hear about her in the Bible was when Abraham's servant came looking for her. Let us consider some backstory for anyone who may not be familiar with Rebecca in the Bible.

### *Rebecca's backstory*

In Genesis chapter 24, Abraham, the patriarch of Israel, needed to find a wife for his son.

Abraham was the man with a covenant with God that his descendants would become an entire nation. To have descendants, of course, his son, Isaac, who God promised would be the ancestor of those descendants, needed to have a wife.

Abraham sent his faithful servant, Eliezer, on a journey to his relatives' homeland so that Eliezer could find a wife for Isaac among Abraham's extended family. Eliezer said a prayer to God for this journey. He asked the Lord that the young woman who was helpful to him, who had no reservations about serving him and his company or camels, should be the one that God had chosen for Isaac.

What a prayer. Abraham's servant was essentially asking for the humblest girl that he could possibly find. A girl who had no issues with serving complete strangers such as him.

Eliezer had uttered this prayer beside a well. He had scarcely finished praying when a young girl came by to fetch water. According to Genesis 24 verse 16, she was very beautiful.

She was the daughter of Abraham's nephew. Eliezer went to her and asked her for a little water. She did not just give him water—she offered, without being asked, to fetch water for his entire team with him or his animals. Eliezer knew that God had provided an immediate answer to his prayer.

This is the first insight that we gain of Rebecca from the Bible. Humble. Helpful. Sympathetic to other people's needs. Eliezer took her back with him to meet Isaac, and she became his wife.

This was when Rebecca's ministry truly started.

## The birth of Esau and Jacob

Rebecca was married for a while but could not become pregnant. Her husband prayed to the Lord about it, and God answered.

It is possible that this may have had a great impression on Rebecca. Note that she came from a home where her family did not believe in the God that Abraham believed in. Abraham had separated from his extended family for many years. He believed God, but his family did not, as would be evidenced later that they served "household gods." Therefore, Rebecca was coming into marriage from a home where her family served idols.

Isaac prayed about her barrenness, and God answered. She became pregnant. For a girl coming from a family where idols were her gods, it would appear that this was a fascinating phenomenon that there is a God that answers prayers in such a unique way. Remember that Eliezer, Abraham's servant, had testified to her family that he prayed at the water well to God, and Rebecca showed up. And now, her husband prayed for her, and she got pregnant!

One may not be certain about her experiences with her household gods back home, but this God of Abraham must have intrigued her. She got bold with going to look for him when she had issues that were bothering her.

For instance, only a few verses after she was described as getting pregnant through prayers, Rebecca discovered that her pregnancy was a troubling one. There was a lot of movement in her womb.

She was not shy about running to pray! She had heard of Eliezer's prayer. She had seen Isaac pray. Surely, there was something about their God! So she went to pray to him.

And God answered, just like he had been doing for Abraham's *household anytime they prayed to Him. God told her audibly about her pregnancy:*

> *[The founders of] two nations are in your womb, and the separation of two peoples has begun in your body; the one people shall be stronger than the other, and the elder shall serve the younger.*
> *When her days to be delivered were fulfilled, behold, there were twins in her womb. (Genesis 25:23–24 AMPC)*

Rebecca had discovered the power behind prayers of inquiry to God. She had discovered how to manage any issues around her household. God had answered her.

When her twins were born, the first child was called Esau, and the second was Jacob. When the children grew up to be adults, the Bible states that Isaac loved Esau, the older, while Rebecca loved Jacob, the younger.

Isaac's reasons for loving Esau over Jacob, his younger son, was revealed. Esau was a hunter, and he always brought good meat for his father! Therefore, Isaac loved him for that.

On the other hand, the Bible narrates that Rebecca preferred Jacob, but there was no further information provided about *why*. He was described as a plain man who lived in tents. There was nothing spectacular about him since he was not a cunning hunter like his brother.

Therefore, why did Rebecca love him?

## *Rebecca's insights about God matters*

If we recall, when Rebecca was pregnant, God had told her that her younger son would be greater than her older son.

God did not appear to have unveiled this detail to Isaac, the children's father.

Thus, Isaac was choosing his favorite child based on the material things that the child could bring to him.

As for Rebecca' choice of favorite child, even though the Bible did not mention why Rebecca preferred Jacob out of her two sons, it seems that the message God had given her before they were born must have played a pivotal role.

God had told her the spiritual position of the two boys. That the younger would be master to the older boy. *The younger was God's favorite.*

Therefore, Rebecca chose God's choice too. The younger son was Rebecca's favorite. She did not seem to struggle with it, or at least, it was not mentioned. She went with God's opinion on who he had allowed to be the greater son.

## *Profile of a female godly leader*

Rebecca is the archetypical example of a leader who was trying to establish God's children into their destinies.

There were some features that made her the kind of woman that God could confide in because, note again, it is possible that God did not tell Isaac about the children's destinies.

Rebecca was the only one who seemed to know that Jacob would be greater. Afterall, why was Isaac preferring his elder son, Esau, for such superficial reasons as the type of meat that Esau could bring to him from each hunting expedition? It must have been because Isaac did not know that he had a greater treasure of a son in the household—his younger son, Jacob.

What are these features that seem to have endeared the Lord to revealing secrets to Rebecca, making her a leader in her household?

*She was humble.* From the days of her youth, it appears that Rebecca was a humble woman. She was the one who went running to fetch water for the servant that asked her for water at the well, thereby, procuring her marital destiny through her humility!

*She took responsibility.* When she did not understand something, she did not depend on her husband to go and fix it. As soon as she knew that the God of Abraham was a prayer-answering God, she took responsibility. She did not wait for Isaac to build a relationship with God on her behalf. It would have been impossible.

She went to build one herself by holding conversations with God. She demonstrated that faith in God is a personal thing, and one does not depend on husband, pastor, or community to do the praying and the pursuing after God for them. It is a personal *cross* to be carried individually.

*She was an inquirer.* When she came to a point of confusion (her pregnancy), she went to ask God about it. There is a passage in the New Testament that God reminds to all:

> *Do not fret or have any anxiety about anything, but in every circumstance and in everything, by prayer and petition (definite requests), with thanksgiving, continue to make your wants known to God. (Philippians 4:6 AMPC)*

Rebecca was a demonstration of a woman who seeks God when she is worried about something. She does not turn to gossip, or complaining, or, in modern times, social media is not her mode of seeking answers.

Perhaps, this is a feature that God is looking for in today's church leaders, including or especially women, since Rebecca was a female leader. He is the God that changes not. Therefore, his standards have not been altered over the centuries. *"For I am the Lord, I do not change" (Malachi 3:6 AMPC)*

*She stuck with God's plan.* As soon as Rebecca discovered that Jacob would be the greater son, she stuck with the plan. God said so, then she might as well follow that trajectory.

A person who knows of God's desires—and works toward it—could be eligible for leadership in God!

## *The synopsis about Rebecca*

There are many other matters to be said about Rebecca. However, this brief glimpse into her leadership qualities may be sufficient for providing some pointers as to the features that made up this type of female leader from the Bible.

The fact that God allowed her to engage in all these activities that followed after his heart's desire—that placed Jacob at the forefront of his destiny—that faithfully followed after what God said, means that maybe, God is not opposed to female leaders serving Him.

Perhaps, as long as they display the qualities that Rebecca possessed, they may have a chance.

There are situations where leaders in the church may sometimes "feel" that they are led to do something for God, yet, the feeling is not from God. It is simply their own desires or expectations about what they should be doing in the church. In such situations, service to God becomes a monumental struggle, and they will not have the ease of divine support.

On the other hand, there are those who God himself endorses. And if they are female, their walk in the ministry, even if challenged, will enjoy a supernatural enablement that ordinary ministries do not experience.

Therefore, in this book on female church leaders, as we progress to the next section of the book, the focal point is really not just about why females should be church leaders, but also, are they approved to take on that office by divine appointment?

The matter of divine appointment is a relevant one. A true minister of God does not take the seat based on "feeling led" to be called. Feelings are nebulous.

Leaders in the Bible were audibly positioned in their roles by direct command from heaven.

Prophet Samuel was expressly commanded by God to make David the king. Elisha was specifically directed by the Lord to anoint Elijah as a prophet. King David was specifically directed by God that, out of his many sons, Solomon alone would be king.

It happened this way, back in Biblical times, that God chooses leaders through announcements from Him directly, and not through human feelings.

The order of how God works His ways of leadership selection has not changed.

> *For I am the Lord, I do not change. (Malachi 3:6 AMPC)*

# PART 2
## The Ministry Experience

In the Old Testament, it is notable that women in leadership positions were few and far between. Thus, the handful of examples that were provided in the previous section of this book demonstrate that, though women were few, they were approved for their positions by God.

In the sections of the book which follow, we will now turn to the happenings of the New Testament.

How were women treated in matters of God and leadership roles after Jesus came to the Earth? Have things changed? Is society truly the culprit that is preventing or limiting women from ministry?

**CHAPTER 5**

# *The Outpouring at Pentecost*

Pentecost was a special day in the New Testament.

As is the tradition with this book, some back story is in order!

## *The days before Pentecost*

Most or all the world has heard about Jesus Christ.

He is the kind of Person that one does not get convinced to believe the things he said of himself or of who he is unless one experiences what he meant by his words, personally.

This is a confusing concept or subject for many as the typical knowledge about Jesus Christ in most circles is an esoteric, cloudy view about someone called the *Son of God* who came to the Earth to save the sins of the world; and if you believe in him, "you will be saved."

There is more to him than this little snippet of popular rhetoric that is so popular in the world!

However, as this book is focusing on women in his church and their gaining leadership positions, the writing will not go into the details of the "who" of Jesus. It is a fundamental discussion, but we will remain with the topic about women and their place in his church this time around!

## *The day of Pentecost—backstory*

The usual process in this book is to consider some backstory. What is Pentecost? If you are a Bible scholar or simply the average Scripture reader, you may be familiar with this term. It probably warrants some introduction so that we may weave it into this narration about Pentecost and its effects on the Christian ministry.

When Jesus lived on the Earth, he promised his disciples that after his resurrection and his departure from Earth, he would send his Holy Spirit to be the helper of anyone who believes in him.

> *But you shall receive power (ability, efficiency, and might) when the Holy Spirit has come upon you, and you shall be My witnesses in Jerusalem and all Judea and Samaria and to the ends (the very bounds) of the earth.*
>
> *And when He (Jesus) had said this, even as they were looking [at Him], He was caught up, and a cloud received and carried Him away out of their sight. (Acts 1:8 AMPC)*

There was a specific day that this event was supposed to take place—the event of the Holy Spirit coming upon them so that they were able to receive a supernatural type of boldness that would enable them to confidently talk about him and the message of the Gospel to anyone and at any location in the world. But he did not tell them *when it would happen.*

On a particular day, this event which Jesus had promised *did* occur. There were about one hundred and twenty of his disciples gathered together in a room. The Bible describes the occurrence that followed as the sound of a "rushing mighty wind" and tongues of fire, appearing on the heads of each individual that was gathered.

In discussions today, it may sound surreal and incredible if such a happening was described to someone in modern-day Earth. However, the results could not be denied that something different had happened to these individuals who had gathered in the upper room on that particular day.

The most tangible difference about the disciples who received a baptism of the Holy Spirit was that they began to speak in other languages instantaneously—languages that they had never learned before. In fact, there was amazement by certain onlookers who knew that some of these people did not have formal education or whatever the equivalent of formal education may have been at 33. Therefore, where had they learnt languages? Or more accurately, how could they have learned such languages within the space of a day?

This is the background story of the Pentecost. It represents the day when the Holy Spirit came upon the disciples of Jesus, and they received an enablement that could not be humanly explained but which allowed them to speak to anyone, with undeniable wisdom, about the things of God, who was considered a controversial topic in those days—and who is still considered a controversial topic today!

The event of the Pentecost was, for interchangeable reference, otherwise known as the "Baptism of the Holy Spirit."

## *Who was Pentecost intended to benefit?*

The baptism happened to all who believed in Jesus and who was gathered in the upper room on that fateful day—both male and female. Their faith was what attracted their becoming baptized.

It is worthy to note that Jesus did not differentiate about who would be *most* enabled by the Holy Spirit's power to become "ministry qualified." He did not indicate that men would be more enabled than women.

It is noteworthy to consider a point from the book of Galatians:

> *For as many [of you] as were baptized into*
> *Christ [into a spiritual union and communion with*
> *Christ, the Anointed One, the Messiah] have put on*
> *(clothed yourselves with) Christ.*
> *There is [now no distinction] neither Jew nor*
> *Greek, there is neither slave nor free, there is not*

*male and female; for you are all one in Christ Jesus.*
*(Galatians 3:27–28 AMPC)*

The baptism into Jesus Christ, which is believing in Jesus, does not discriminate between male and female. This chapter is going to make an attempt to focus on what happened to the females that were or who became part of the church after the Day of Pentecost.

Were they active leaders?

Did they pursue leadership positions? Or were they content to sit in the sidelines and background while the men took the lead on growing the church?

If so, why did they take a back seat?

## The measure

The answer to the questions about why women may have a back seat in churches in ancient times and today may not be a mystery.

God gave the Holy Spirit to all believers equally. However, the increase of grace, the ability to walk with God, the improvement in character, the changes to lifestyle, and the transformation of a person's mind to become the type of mind that God can use is wholly dependent on the individual. These activities are known as "works"—something that God requires that a person should have as a complement to their faith.

"Works" of faith will inevitably lead to transformation of the mind. A person who receives Jesus as Savior will experience a change, over time, that will evidentially demonstrate to the person and the people around them that their behaviors, the way they think, and the experiences they have in life are no longer the same as previously before they accepted Christ.

*Do not be conformed to this world (this age),*
*[fashioned after and adapted to its external, super-*
*ficial customs], but be transformed (changed) by*
*the [entire] renewal of your mind. (Romans 12:2*
*AMPC)*

This raises the question: If mind transformation, increase in grace, and all other works of faith are the responsibility of the individual—and if people like Apostle Paul worked at it so diligently that even demons began to recognize him as a man of power—then why are there no similar testimonies of women in the New Testament church of the Bible?

Were there no women pursuing their faith as vigorously as Apostle Paul did? Or like Peter?

Scripture reminds us: God is no respecter of persons.

> *Most certainly and thoroughly I now perceive*
> *and understand that God shows no partiality and is*
> *no respecter of persons. (Acts 10:34 AMPC)*

Thus, the only conclusion to this question is that women may not have pursued ministry as hard as the men did because of the culture of the day in Biblical times.

They left the heavier lifting to the men because this was the tradition.

To any woman who is reading this book: Now that we have confirmed that God is no respecter of persons and if there was a mighty Apostle Paul and there can also be a mighty Apostle Paula, only if she works her faith as hard as Paul did, maybe it is time for women in the modern age to work harder at their faith—and then the confirmation or anointing for bigger opportunities in God will come to them.

# CHAPTER 6

# Women Who Believed

In the book of Acts, there were some women who seemed to take the spotlight as representatives of females in the ministry: As examples, Mary, the mother of Jesus; Tabitha, also known as Dorcas; Priscilla; and Lydia.

*Mary, the mother of Jesus—backstory*

There may be a few people that have wondered: Why Mary? Why was she chosen to be Jesus's mother?

Israel was a nation of millions—at least, it seems this is what "multitudes" mean. As an example, the army of King David, one of the foremost and probably the best rulers of Israel, had an army according to the following numbers, *even before he became king*. His army:

> *Those of Judah, who bore shield and spear,*
> *were 6,800 armed for war;*
> *Those of Simeon, mighty and brave warriors,*
> *7,100;*
> *Those of Levi, 4,600—*
> *Jehoiada…with him were 3,700,*
> *Of the Benjamites, the kindred of [King] Saul,*
> *3,000—*

*Of the Ephraimites, 20,800;*
*Of the half-tribe of Manasseh, 18,000;*
*Of Zebulun, 50,000 experienced troops;*
*Of Naphtali, 1,000 captains, and with them*
37,000 *with shield and spear;*
*Of Dan, 28,600;*
*Of Asher…40,000;*
*…of Reuben and Gad and the half-tribe*
*of Manasseh, 120,000 men, armed with all the*
*weapons and instruments of war. (1 Chronicles*
*12:24–37)*

Israel experienced some turbulence in the years following King David's reign; they were dispersed among other nations and lost their land for a while. They eventually returned to rebuild their lost homeland. The reason why the army numbers of David's men were recited above was to provide a glimpse of how many and how mighty Israel was as a nation when the army of a man, who was not yet king, could be that numerous.

This does not take us away from the discussion about Mary.

The reason why Israel's numbers was demonstrated above was to highlight that Mary was just one "insignificant" girl in the midst of a numerous and vast people.

Why was she chosen to become the mother of Jesus? What did God see in her? Obviously, he could not choose a man for this job. A woman was needed because she was to become pregnant and have a unique child by immaculate conception.

Why was Mary the leading lady for this role?

There is a verse in Scripture that mentions:

*Man looks at the outward appearance, God*
*looks at the heart. (1 Samuel 16:7)*

There have been multiple literary pieces about Mary, about her being the Mother of Jesus Christ and about her relationship with Joseph, her future husband.

Has anyone wondered about her story before she became chosen to be the mother of Jesus? Surely, a lot of things must have happened in her life before marital age rolled around, and she was facing the prospect of becoming a mother to the Lord Jesus!

There was something about Mary's heart. As previously indicated in an earlier scripture, "God looks at the heart." One can picture it like this: When God Almighty is viewing humanity, he is not looking at race. Or height (Eliab the tall army officer, rejected as king). Or social status (Joseph the slave, who became a ruler). Or eloquence (Moses the stammerer, who led Israel out of slavery).

He sees men as *hearts*. Thus, if two people are standing side by side, and they were being observed from the eyes of God, he is identifying them by their hearts. Is the heart of that one vengeful? Is it foolishly angry? Is it too arrogant to be rebuked or corrected?

God disqualifies men—and women—from godly positions, by reasons of heart matters.

Perhaps, this is the reason why, despite three and a half years of intense ministry on Earth, Jesus had only 120 people that gathered in the room in Jerusalem on the Day of Pentecost. The hearts of only 120 people in an entire nation were ready for God at that particular point in time.

Thus, what can we say about Mary's heart?

Out of a multitude of women in Israel, young girls, beautiful, and available, Mary was the only one that passed whatever test God may have applied to the nation of Israel to select her for the very important position of mother of Jesus.

Looking through the Bible, one can tell that there are certain qualities about a person which makes God to notice them.

*Rebecca*—She had the heart of a servant, the real, unpretentious type that goes out of the way to help strangers without expecting a reward.

*Joseph*—He had a heart of focus. Even as a slave, he never stopped using his gift of interpreting dreams.

*Moses*—He had the heart of a prince while the rest of his people believed they were slaves.

*Deborah*—She had a heart that did not despise small roles. She was a housewife helping other housewives or resolving domestic disputes before God promoted her to a rank of national adviser or advising the military general of Israel.

*David*—He had an insatiable heart hunger for knowledge of God, which is very different from knowledge *about* God.

Since the Lord, historically, had liked the people who had hearts as described above, there is a possibility that Mary may have possessed some or all the qualities mentioned.

## Mary's life as Mother of Jesus

After considering Mary's backstory, the time seems ripe to think about her female leadership opportunities or qualifications. Would the Bible have considered her a leader?

She had a heart to be selected as mother of Jesus.

As a church leader—probably not.

This would be a very controversial statement, especially among certain denominations of the Christian faith.

However, think about it for a moment, from the perspective of an intelligent God, who is very calculative in choosing people. Consider what Jesus said about Mary and his brothers when they came to see him while he was going about, preaching:

> *While Jesus was still talking to the crowd, his mother and brothers stood outside, wanting to speak to him.*
>
> *Someone told him, "Your mother and brothers are standing outside, wanting to speak to you."*
>
> *He replied to him, "Who is my mother, and who are my brothers?"*
>
> *Pointing to his disciples, he said, "Here are my mother and my brothers.*
>
> *For whoever does the will of my Father in heaven is my brother and sister and mother." (Matthew 12:46–49)*

There is reason to wonder: Why did Jesus have to mention that "whoever does the will of his Father would be his brother, sister, and mother?"

It would appear that Mary qualified to be his mom, but in terms of an office in his ministry, she did not have one. She was a back seater. If she had "leveraged" her position as mother of the son of God, like Esther did as queen, Mary would have been more visible than the cursory mentions in the Bible after Jesus was born.

Or maybe God did not want her in a visible role? This may be a possibility. Yet Jesus's rebuke about those who can be his mother or brethren may indicate that he had expected more from her for she already had the position of honor given to her by appointment

What *will* of God was Mary not following that Jesus had to make mention of those who were truly his mother, sister, and brother in Matthew 12?

It may be that she lived a comfortable, stay-at-home life, while Jesus walked through cities, preaching. The fact that she came to visit him along with his brothers in the passage of scripture of Matthew 12 would demonstrate that she did not really follow him from city to city for his ministry.

The reason why Mary's is being mentioned as someone who could-have-been-a-better influential person in Jesus's ministry is to point out that there was so much potential for her to have been a huge mention in the Bible if she had acted out followership of Jesus rather than simply relaxed in the role of his mother.

"Acting out followership" of Jesus can be seen from the examples of his disciples: They fully used the status of "these men have been with Jesus" to validate their being able to get into synagogues or gain preaching opportunities. Of course, God helped them. Yet imagine the degree of leadership potential that Mary could have accomplished by being the mother of Jesus, who openly talked about it in the marketplace. It is true that women did not have a voice like men did back in those days.

Yet it is also true that there were women who did not stay bound by those limitations and did what men could do anyway because they already had the appointment from God himself. It is one thing to take a back seat because God has not audibly told one that he has an official role for them. But for those already appointed by God into an office, like Mary, what is that female's excuse?

Mariam went to observe what happened to her little brother, Moses, when he was placed in a basket on the Nile. Her brother, Aaron, was the eldest. Why did he not step in to do it instead? Because Miriam may have been more convicted, and her female status did not deter her from taking up that ministry for her little brother to ensure no harm came to him. Did her parents stop her from going to look out for Moses because she was a girl?

No. She did a small act in her level of status as a little girl. She was not looking for a position. Just doing what she could to save a soul in her little world. God elevated her to prophetess as the years went by.

Deborah openly judged, something that only men had been doing before her. Did any man stop her because she was a woman?

No. She filled her little role, judging domestic disputes under a tree, and God gave her a big appointment out of it.

The bottom line about the story of Mary is this: *A female leader appointed by God already has his backing and leverage to be used by him. If she is not stepping out, it is unfortunate.*

Esther had a whole chapter to herself, and she was only a queen, not as highly placed as Mary's role, which was the mother of the Son of God.

## Tabitha's backstory

Tabitha was first mentioned in Acts chapter 9 from verse 36.

The book of Acts does not say much about her beyond this chapter. One can deduce from "she was always doing good and helping the poor" that she was literally walking in the footsteps of Jesus.

> *How God anointed and consecrated Jesus of Nazareth with the [Holy] Spirit and with strength and ability and power; how He went about doing good. (Acts 10:38 AMPC)*

Further, Jesus specifically spoke about the core of his ministry in Isaiah 61:

> *The Spirit of the Lord God is upon me, because the Lord has anointed and qualified me to preach the Gospel of good tidings to the meek, the poor, and afflicted. (Isaiah 61:1 AMPC)*

Tabitha was doing good, and she was helping the poor. It was like stepping into Jesus's footprints. It would appear that she was not just doing it as an empty act because she was authentic enough to impact her entire community. So much so that when she died, an urgent message had to be sent to Peter that he needed to come to her city for an emergency.

## A woman of impact

A read-through of Acts 9 from verses 36 to 38 reveals that Tabitha was impactful.

That is what ministry is about.

Ministry is not about a title.

It is not about being recognized, for instance, on a pulpit.

It is about *followership*. This appears to be what God recognizes as a true leader. It is incidental that such a follower would climb up on a pulpit or to a visible role in a church to lead its people.

Ministry begins in the secret place of a person's life, in the community where "little deeds" are impacting lives, just like Tabitha was doing.

If there are not many women in the visible pulpit arena, the question is probably not about whether they are being prevented by traditions and by society from rising to the pulpit. Afterall, the current society is more modern than the days of the Bible. Women are, today, taking on reins that only men had taken, historically.

The question of why there are fewer women in ministry is whether the women have applied themselves to *followership* so that there is no doubt that God has appointed them to preach on pulpits because they *followed someone else in ministry.*

It seems that such an attitude would be considered as important to God's heart and whether he decides to bring such a woman to any of his pulpits.

The bottom line is: if it is God himself that anoints a woman to work in public office for the church, there is no human that can stop it, not even traditional biases or attempts to disqualify her.

## *Priscilla's backstory*

Priscilla is mentioned in several books of the Bible!

She was mentioned in Acts 18, Romans 16, 1 Corinthians 16, and 2 Timothy 4. She was always named side by side with Aquila, her husband.

This testimony reveals something right off the bat about the type of woman that Priscilla was—or at least the impression that the Bible wanted to leave about her.

She was a "Proverbs 31 woman" or a woman who was close to her husband! They were always together. Even though she was living in the first century, and perhaps, women were more submissive or subjected to forced obedience, it is doubtful that she was being forced to always appear with her husband on the scene of anywhere that the Bible mentioned her.

For anyone who may not be familiar with Proverbs 31, here are the highlights:

> *A capable, intelligent, and virtuous woman— who is he who can find her? She is far more precious than jewels and her value is far above rubies or pearls.*
>
> *The heart of her husband trusts in her confidently and relies on and believes in her securely, so that he has no lack of [honest] gain or need of [dishonest] spoil.*

> *She comforts, encourages, and does him only*
> *good as long as there is life within her. (Proverbs 31:*
> *10–12)*

Notice the first thing that was mentioned about Priscilla in Acts 18:24–26 in the following paragraphs.

## *Priscilla and Aquila*

There was a Jew called Apollos, educated and very fervent in his zeal to preach. He preached boldly in the synagogue, but his message was focused on baptism by John the Baptist, who is identified as the prophet that came to announce Jesus's coming in the same generation that Jesus came to the Earth.

The Bible says that "Priscilla and Aquilas" heard him, and they invited him to their home to explain to him the way of God more adequately.

Priscilla and Aquilas did this *together*. They properly discipled a soul for the kingdom of God as a couple.

If Apostle Paul, the man who wrote practically half of the New Testament, could make a worthy mention of Priscilla and Aquila in his letters, they must have been very impactful indeed. Paul wrote to the church in Rome:

> *Greet Priscilla and Aquila, my co-workers in*
> *Christ Jesus. They risked their lives for me. (Romans*
> *16:3–4 AMPC)*

It seems that the point of Priscilla being mentioned in the Bible is that a woman's ministry is not disqualified if she is doing it side by side with her husband.

Being solo at the pulpit as a female minister does not make it more glamorous. Doing it together with her husband makes it stronger. For "*two are stronger than one because they have a good return for their labor*" (Ephesians 4:9).

There is no doubt that Priscilla and Aquilla ran a church together, in their house, according to the Biblical account:

*Aquila and Prisca, together with the church [that meets] in their house, send you their hearty greetings in the Lord. (1 Corinthians 16:19)*

Thus, in the argument for women in ministry, this particular aspect of reality should be considered. She is a strong woman for being able to work with her husband in matters of ministry, and besides, he needs her more than she probably needs him to succeed!

Afterall, *"the heart of her husband trusts in her confidently and relies on her" (Proverbs 31).*

## Lydia's backstory

Lydia was a very brief mention in the book of Acts. Her actions represent a woman who was proactive.

In Acts chapter 16, Paul and his son-in-the Lord, Timothy, went to sit by the riverside in a Roman colony district. Several local women were gathered there. They began to have a conversation with them, of course, about the matters of Jesus, and God's heart for the world on salvation.

The women listened to the things that Paul and Timothy had to say. This is where Lydia was introduced as one of the women. Consider one of the first impressions that was provided about her:

*She was a worshipper of God. (Acts 16: 14)*

## Who is a worshipper?

The Bible's perspective on those who are worshippers of God, as opposed to merely Christians by designation, are the individuals who worship God "in spirit and in truth."

> *God is a Spirit (a spiritual Being) and those*
> *who worship Him must worship Him in spirit and*
> *in truth (reality). (John 4:24)*

As the Bible qualifies and interprets itself by referring to something mentioned in one part with something else mentioned in other parts, we can conclude that Lydia's being a worshipper of God is interpreted in John 4:24 to mean that she was a worshipper of God "in spirit and in truth."

It may mean that she made quite an impression on the Lord so that "worshipper" was one of the first characteristics remembered concerning her before other features were introduced.

For this reason, it would appear that a woman who wants to be recognized, not by men, but by God himself for leadership roles or simply for being true to him would need to fit this description of a "worshipper in spirit and in truth."

## *A woman of trade*

Lydia was a worshipper of God, but she was also a businesswoman.

There have been views in modern times that a woman who is truly serving God would be one that shuns the "unholy" business of the secular world, focusing one hundred percent of her attention on ministry matters.

Lydia was a merchant—a businesswoman. *A dealer.*

> *A woman named Lydia, from the city of*
> *Thyatira, a dealer in fabrics dyed in purple. (Acts*
> *16:14)*

The conclusion then is that being an active business person does not exclude a woman from the platform of ministry of people or minister to God.

Lydia was accepted by God for an honorable mention because it was confirmed that the Lord opened her heart to pay attention to what was said by Paul. It is possible that there were other women in that gathering whose hearts were not open to this message. It would be evidence that God did not reach out to help those other particular women accept a message that was new and, maybe even disturbing, because of something of the heart they did not have in them—which Lydia did.

## The "disturbing" Gospel

It would be necessary to mention the possibility that the gospel was not accepted by all in the time of Jesus Christ on Earth—and this continues to be the same in present day.

The woman who is able to accept news that is uncommon, maybe even new, or that challenges her prior beliefs would probably be a woman like Lydia—a woman whose heart is opened by God to be able to believe anything about him, even if it is offensive to others.

How do we know a woman who is cut out for ministry? She is the one that hears the gospel, the type of gospel that Jesus preached, which made people angry enough to crucify him, and yet, that woman, cut out for ministry, would continue to believe him. For if people were angry about the gospel at the turn of the first century, there may potentially be those, even of the household of Christianity, who are angry about some of its assertions in our modern-day world as well.

A woman of ministry would need to have a heart that can withstand the rejections of people being offended at the true gospel of Jesus while her own heart accepts the unusual testimonies that it gives.

Such a woman would be the type of woman of ministry that God is looking for.

Lydia appears to be this kind of woman.

## Deference

There was something unusual and impactful that Lydia said after hearing Paul and Timothy preaching. The events went as follows:

> *And when she was baptized along with her household, she earnestly entreated us (Paul and*

*Timothy), saying, If in your opinion I am one really convinced [that Jesus is the Messiah and the Author of salvation] and that I will be faithful to the Lord, come to my house and stay. (Acts 16:15 AMPC)*

What a woman!

She asked for the opinion of the apostles regarding whether she was someone "convinced" about Jesus and whether they considered she would be faithful to the Lord. In other words, she was asking whether they thought she was a good candidate for Jesus's ministry.

Most Christians would not consider the opinions of spiritual authorities in the church about whether they are "good candidates" for anything in God. They may simply think they can decide on it themselves. Apparently, this is not the way the early church operated. The opinions of the church authorities—the authorities ordained by God—appear to have mattered.

As warned in the course of this writing, some of these perspectives may be offensive. However, this may be the reason why the church does not have many people that are truly endorsed by God himself into ministerial offices.

## *The topic of women in ministry*

In considering the topic of women in ministry, it is essential to look at all possible facets, not just the argument that "men are the only ones that have been in ministry, and they are excluding women."

Rather, the various pieces that involve true ministry—for instance, followership (mentioned in Mary's story), humility (mentioned in Rebecca's story), worshipful heart (mentioned in Lydia's story), and the other characteristics that each Biblical woman brought to the table—should be part of the review.

**CHAPTER 7**

# The Gifts of the Holy Spirit

A ministry cannot function in the Biblical way without the gifts of the Holy Spirit. What are these?

*Description of the gifts*

There is a long passage in the Bible about gifts of the Spirit in the book of 1 Corinthians. Note the various types of gifts identified in bold:

> *To one is given in and through the [Holy] Spirit **[the power to speak] a message of wisdom**, and to **another [the power to express] a word of knowledge and understanding** according to the same [Holy] Spirit;*
>
> *To another **[wonder-working] faith** by the same [Holy] Spirit, to another the **extraordinary powers of healing** by the one Spirit;*
>
> *To another the **working of miracles**, to another **prophetic insight (the gift of interpreting the divine will and purpose)**; to another the **ability to discern and distinguish** between [the utterances of true] spirits [and false ones], to*

> ***another various kinds of [unknown] tongues**, to
> another **the ability to interpret [such] tongues**.
> All these [gifts, achievements, abilities] are
> inspired and brought to pass by one and the same
> [Holy] Spirit, Who apportions to each person indi-
> vidually [exactly] as He chooses. (1 Corinthian
> 12:8–11 AMPC)*

There are nine gifts that are identified in the book of Corinthians. It seems that each believer would have received a measure of one or more of these gifts, which is mentioned in 1 Corinthians 12:7. It could be that a believer is not yet fully "functional" unless they have a gift of the Spirit as it is the evidence that they have believed in Jesus Christ.

This chapter will focus on gifts of the Spirit and its impact on the potential of women-led ministries.

## All working together

There is a key message in the book of 1 Corinthians that ties the experience of the gifts of the Spirit together with working in church, literally. There needs to be a "working as one."

> *So that there should be no division or discord
> or lack of adaptation [of the parts of the body to
> each other], but the members all alike should have
> a mutual interest in and care for one another. (1
> Corinthians 12:25)*

The proper foundation for a ministry, including a female-led one, to begin blossoming is a foundation of unity.

The church where there are divisions about whether a female was bypassed for a leadership post in the church—or whether women are being excluded as key parts in decision making in ministries—represents an environment where such female who is seeking ministry recognition or opportunity will likely not get a true, God-inspired one. One of the features that is often lauded about God, about Jesus, and about the Holy Spirit is that he is a God of peace.

The God of peace would not be involved in a contest or dissensions among church members about who has been excluded from a post and quarrels or hard feelings that may result from those disagreements.

Moreover, if he is not involved, could that be the reason why people, including women, who may have had the opportunity to be endorsed by him, may never receive it because they engage in controversies about unequal treatments of the genders?

There is something that seems surreal, but which is the reality, based on Biblical testaments. The ways and thoughts under which God operates is very different from the ways and thoughts of humans. Ostensibly, the passage in Scripture that testifies of this says that "his ways are higher than our ways."

If his Spirit is the one who is performing acts in the church and there is a requirement that unity must exist in order for his Spirit to act among believers, it seems impossible, by his standards then, that he would be in support of gender wars and dissensions regarding why women are not being placed in ministry as much as men.

Hence, we have a conundrum. If women are not well represented in ministerial work and divisions exist in the church because of this—and God will not get involved in *endorsing* anyone for offices, male or female, while they are in the midst of disagreements—then what could be the potential way out to resolve the matter of women having their fair chance in church ministries as leaders?

## *How to be a female leader in God*

*Stop seeking leadership positions.* This is an oxymoron. The Bible testifies of several examples where those who were avoiding positions in God were the specific ones that he wanted to choose because they did not consider themselves "worthy" for such posts. He was the one who made the decision for them as their hearts were humble.

Consider a few examples. These individuals in the Bible, though not female examples, expressed how unworthy they were for the positions that God kept handing out to them. If the chapters are read in full, one will notice that the Lord had to convince them to take the darn blessing of the position he was handing out, which they did not want!

*Example One:*

When the Lord was trying to send Moses as the leader to deliver Israel from slavery.

> And he (Moses) said, Oh, my Lord, I pray
> You, *send by the hand of [some other]* whom You
> will [send]. (Exodus 4:13)

*Example Two:*

When the Lord was personally selecting Gideon to be the army general that would deliver Israel from their enemies.

> Gideon said to Him, Oh Lord, how can I
> deliver Israel? Behold, my clan is the poorest in
> Manasseh, and *I am the least in my father's house."*
> (Judges 6:15)

*Example Three:*

David's self-recrimination when God wanted to make him a prince through marriage.

> David said to Saul, *Who am I, and what is*
> *my life or my father's family in Israel, that I should*
> *be the king's son-in-law?* (1 Samuel 18:18)

*Let God do the choosing.* Having *feelings* about going into ministry are very different from actually getting sent by God himself.

If the examples of real leaders in the Bible is not convincing enough about how God selects leaders himself, it is worth mentioning here.

Without attempting to discourage anyone from a ministry oath, a true leader of God is not stepping into a bed of roses when God endorses them. There are wars to fight. There are souls to win. There are rejections to endure. All in one day's work.

Most individual's emotional stamina cannot endure the true requirements of a God-ordained leader. Consider Apostle Paul. Consider Apostle Peter. While today's persecutions may not lead to a church leader being crucified or murdered like they were, the experience of the true work of a God-ordained office is not a light matter.

Maybe this is why God *endorses* only a very few while there are a multitude of other church posts that are founded by humans on "feelings of going into ministry" as opposed to God's endorsement driving it.

## Confirmations of ministry

If God is the one that would choose his own leaders by himself as opposed to individuals taking ministerial offices without his confirming it, how does a person know whether they have an office confirmation from God, especially a woman?

The best answer to this is to refer back to the females already discussed in this book.

*Rebecca:* She was not looking for a position as an ancestor to the great nation that birthed Christ, yet she was chosen because she was going about her normal life, serving strangers in the process, such as Abraham's servant.

*Deborah:* She was not seeking any promotions beyond helping to solve petty household disputes, which may be a position that is disdained in our present world. But she proved herself to be dependable in her lowly state so that God started to speak through her about national matters. She did not go seeking it. God came to use her himself.

*Esther:* She was living a normal life in her uncle's house as an orphan. The king's men came to get her, along with other beautiful young women in the district, and she ended up becoming the queen of Persia.

There are other examples that can be mentioned of leaders chosen by God perhaps because they were not seeking it. The unifying factor between them is that these females were not looking for jobs in God. God came looking for them to employ them.

## *Tying confirmation to gifts*

This chapter started out in a discussion about Gifts of the Spirit. It mentioned some themes about how God would not operate in an environment of contention or hard feelings due to being excluded from church offices.

The confirmation into a church position will happen for the individual who is at peace with wherever they are at the moment. They are contentedly operating in whatever gift that God has given them—perhaps encouragement or interpretation of tongues or knowledge and understanding. Or any of the other gifts of the Spirit.

They are going about their relationship with God and not indulging in conflicts of office selections. They are not moved by whether they are female and passed over for church positions.

They know that if God has a post for them that He will personally confirm, there is no one that can prevent it, not even a human political upheaval in the church.

Afterall, with regards to a woman gaining a ministerial public office to serve him and how it could possibly happen to her, thus says the Lord:

> *Surely, as I have thought and planned, so shall*
> *it come to pass, and as I have purposed, so shall it*
> *stand.* (Isaiah 14:24)

# CHAPTER 8
## Ministry

The previous chapter talked about allowing God to do the choosing for the offices that he wants to give to anyone—including women.

It may appear from the prior writing in this book that the female is supposed to sit around and either wait to see if God will choose them for offices or ignore the potential of ministry and go about their lives, and maybe, who knows, God may choose them?

Maybe.

The reality—while they are not pursuing after church opportunities, three is a caveat to add. They are also not idle in their moments or days of obscurity when no position has been confirmed to them.

*Worthy mentions*

Some notable examples of what women were doing in their regular church lives in the New Testament are mentioned here.

Dorcas, an example from a prior chapter, went about "doing good works," a mirror image of what Jesus was described as doing while he was on Earth (Acts 9:36).

The daughters of Philip the evangelist could prophesy and must have been valuable assets for the church in providing inspired utterances (which are not required to be done from a public arena) (Acts 21:8–9).

Priscilla and Aquila had a home church and were said to "risk their lives for Paul" while conducting their little, private home church. (Romans 16:3–4). Further, they were teachers behind the scenes. Priscilla and Aquila were said to have taught the Biblical scholar, Apollos in Acts 18.

Phoebe was described as a "helper" to many so that those she helped would not experience suffering (Romans 16:2).

None of these positions could be described as "glamorous." They are pretty low key, relative to the "action" that Apostle Paul, Apostle Peter, and John the Revelator experienced.

These were ministries of a different kind, with different administrations by the Holy Spirit, no matter how "small" the ministry may be just as the book of *1 Corinthian 12:8–11* mentioned in the previous chapter that there are different gifts of the Spirit.

The mindset about ministry is best explained by realizing that no matter where a person or a woman in Christ finds herself today or the size of their community, they do, in fact, have a ministry already.

There are activities to probably be engaging within the little ministry of their community to make it viable and effective. Like Deborah, if found faithful in the little space, it is possible that the Lord may promote one to something bigger in his timing or according to his will.

Following will be a consideration of the things a woman should be doing while living in "obscurity" or waiting for what God has for her life.

*Prayers*

There seem to be fewer opportunities for prayers in many churches. With the activities of potlucks and weddings and concert planning and other events and happenings, church members are quite busy. The core of what keeps the church centered in thinking of God is often forgotten because of these "busyness" of church life. Prayer becomes a boring drag while the "busyness" takes priority.

There are multiple reasons why prayers are a necessity. Some examples of what prayer was able to perform in the Bible:

Prayers stop plagues or sicknesses:

> *The Lord heeded the prayers for the land, and
> Israel's plague was stayed. (1 Samuel 24:25 AMPC)*

Prayers cause God to defend a person from wrong:

> *Hear their prayer and their supplication in
> heaven, Your dwelling place, and defend their cause
> and maintain their right. (1 Kings 8:49 AMPC)*

Prayers are intended for making a demand to heaven for something that is needed on Earth:

> *In every circumstance and in everything, by
> prayer and petition (definite requests), with thanks-
> giving, continue to make your wants known to God.
> (Phil 4:6 AMPC)*

Most essentially, prayer is necessary for direction. A simple prayer of "Lord, *who am I?*" is a powerful plea that could unveil whether a woman is destined for ministry if she persists at such supplication until God himself answers.

## Giving

There is a ministry called "giving." It is probably one of the toughest tests to anyone that is a believer, especially one who wants to lead in a ministry.

When God was trying to express his love for humankind, he *gave* as can be experienced from the verse:

> *For God so greatly loved and dearly prized
> the world that He [even] gave up His only begotten
> (unique) Son… (John 3:16 AMPC)*

Giving is one of the love languages of the Lord. A person who can give cheerfully is a person that he loves above the regular love that he has "for the world."

Giving is not about donating one's time by serving in a church, although this type of giving is also included.

The real test of giving is financial. It is an area of controversy in many communities regarding churches and the monies that its members give. It is sometimes suggested that the donations to many churches are benefiting the pastors or leaders of the church only.

This may be true for a number of places, but this is not true for any church that was founded by God himself.

## A church founded by God

A God-founded church is different. Its leadership definitely would have a certain type of spiritual gift or more. They are often very focused on the goal and community work, or gatherings is not their main program. Evangelism and soul winning are the core of what they spend their ministry time with doing.

A person who gives to such a church would be enriching their own personal destinies as givers.

## The woman that gives

A person, especially a woman, who is waiting on the Lord and is giving, regardless of controversial topics about giving, would have a focus. Her focus would be that she is giving unto the Lord and not to a collection basket or a pastor. Whatever happens to the money after it leaves her purse is not a thought that will occur to her again. It is like turning your back on the money that used to be in your wallet. The mindset is that God took it from you with his own hand. Therefore, it is in the right place, safe, and no matter what physical recommendations are being made about its use, the woman who gives cheerfully does not care.

She gave unto the Lord.

Even better if such a woman would give "all that she has." This does not mean she would empty out her bank account (although this has happened in a true story before, with incredible endings to that story of the things that began to occur in the giver's life); the woman who gives "all" is giving beyond her measure, and this really attracts God. For instance, if she has a thousand dollars in the bank that is performing no function, giving five dollars out of it is not considered to be a real "giving" from Biblical perspective.

## The story of Abraham

The father of Israel, Abraham, was said to have been told by God: "Take your only son Isaac, to a mountain that I will show you, and sacrifice him to Me there" (Genesis 22:2).

That sounded like a very horrible assignment. It sounded like Abraham was going to give up something he could never recover again. It sounded like God was extremely selfish to be asking him to give up the most precious possession he had.

Therefore, the most logical thing for Abraham to do, if thinking from the mind of God, was to give up Isaac. It is the opposite of how a human being thinks.

The result of his almost-sacrifice was that God told him to stop the act before he could harm the boy and swore that he, the Lord, would bless Abraham with the type of blessings that bring more blessings; and the type of multiplication that brings more multiplication (Genesis 22:17).

The morale of the story: It seems like giving to God's true churches. In other words, churches that he is personally supervising, like Abraham's family, is a "theft" according to modern-day interpretations. It feels like God is taking away from someone.

The controversial answer is: it actually is not.

For the woman who is seeking a place in God, extraordinary giving would be a part of her life.

## *Soul winning*

The final point in ministry—the most important one—is soul winning.

The reason why Jesus came to the planet was for the purpose of winning souls for the kingdom of God. Souls are the heart of God. He would go to amazing lengths to save a human soul from destruction.

Unfortunately, this amazing news is not well understood or believed by majority of the Earth. This is why there is a huge work ahead for a ministry that is deeply into soul winning—not to be confused with mission trips.

Soul winning is something that a woman, who is a true minister of God, would do in her backyard. It represents acts that she would perform for people who may not deserve it just to show them she can treat them differently from others. Soul winning is a sense of urgency about the number of people that are suffering because they have not yet entered into that place of real fellowship with God, where the world has become truly and actually theirs to command as God promised.

Command is a topic for another book.

## *The diagnosis*

Prayer, giving, and soul wining—these are a triple dose of ministerial work that has the potential to birth a ministry for anyone, including and especially a woman who may not consider herself as someone who could have the opportunity.

There is a lot of opportunity for female ministry. Unfortunately, these opportunities are not being considered in the right mindset or at the right places, thereby leading to a lot of lost potential in God by women who could have been ministering in ways and areas that they overlooked because of seeking the "bigger mantle" of ministry work.

The ministry does not begin at the pulpit. In fact, most essential ministries are not pulpit-based.

The woman should not be hung up on pulpit ministries or spotlight opportunities. The greatest examples of the Bible were the seemingly small positions that performed mighty things in God for God performed divine promotions on their works, even in the absence of human-made positions for them.

The greatest examples of mighty ministries are the Deborahs—sitting under trees and resolving domestic disputes. They are the Davids—forgotten in the wilderness and keeping sheep. They are the Josephs—locked up in prison and serving prisoners.

Each one of these did not actively seek a position in ministry. Instead, God was the one who actively sought them out.

In the race for ministerial positions in the church, the latter option (God doing the seeking of who he will appoint) is the glorious and most rewarding one.

# CHAPTER 9
## Contradictions

*Let a woman learn in silence with all submission. And I do not permit a woman to teach or to have authority over a man, but to be in silence.*

—1 Timothy 2:11–12

There are multiple concepts that have been shared in this book about women in ministry or women taking up leadership positions in the church.

### The chapters so far

In chapter 1, Deborah's story was considered and her position as a judge in Israel was analyzed. God did not have a problem with appointing her because she had been faithful in the little things, such as resolving little domestic disputes for his people.

In chapter 2, Miriam, Moses' older sister, was the topic of the section, with a consideration of her role in saving Moses' life, and the fact that she must have taken the initiative to do it. Thus, she had a feature of boldness, which is an absolute requirement for anyone that God would consider for a ministerial position.

In chapter 3, Queen Esther was the story of the day. Selected to be a queen, the pivotal point in her story when she became a true leader of Israel was when she was willing to literally die in the process of making an attempt to see the king and plead her people's case.

She demonstrated the example of a woman who did not care for her life—even to the death. Such is very uncommon in ministry today.

In chapter 4, Rebecca's story unveiled her background as an idol worshipper, who came to see that the God of Isaac was a God who answered prayers, and so she began to follow him. Her story represents the feature of a relentless inquirer of God's will, which God must be looking for in a leader or a woman.

In chapter 5, there was a review of the Pentecost: The mighty event when the Holy Spirit first made himself known to the early church by baptizing them with the evidence of speaking in tongues. This fifth chapter emphasized that the baptism of the Holy Spirit and the benefits of being a disciple of Jesus was not recognized as belonging to any particular gender for God gave it to both male and female.

The results of what a male or female does for increasing in grace in God with what they have been given is entirely up to them.

In chapter 6, there was a walkthrough with the examples of women in the New Testament and their practices of faith.

A consideration of Mary, mother of Jesus Christ, placed her in a unique position of having attracted God's attention due to however she had been living her life before she was called to become Jesus's mother. There was a review of how Mary may have comported herself after Jesus's ministry began and when his work on Earth was done. She did not leverage her position as his mother to do the kind of works that could have earned her greater mentions in the Bible among the hall of fame of Jews, like Apostle Paul or Queen Esther.

The life of Tabitha was discussed in this same chapter, the woman who was "always doing good and helping the poor." She was extremely impactful in her community so that when she died, the people urgently called on Apostle Peter, and it would seem that their desire was that they wanted Peter to perform a work of God that would bring Tabitha back to life!

If a community has an opinion about a person that clearly indicates they would go to such lengths to keep her with them, then what a mighty ministry Tabitha must have had among them that they could not bear to lose her.

Priscilla's story was reviewed in the same chapter, and she brought a different flavor to the view of women in ministry—she was always beside her husband in everything she did for God. Every mention of Priscilla's name always seemed to be attached to the mention of her husband's name, Aquila, as if the Bible recognized them as inseparable.

This particular example of a woman leader of faith provided a reminder that women seeking ministerial positions should not forget the option of ministry which includes their husbands.

As a matter of fact, this may be the choice that God prefers because he is of the view that "two are better than one."

> *Two are better than one, because they have*
> *a good [more satisfying] reward for their labor.*
> *(Ecclesiastes 4: 9 AMPC)*

Of course, one cannot forget Lydia, mentioned in the same chapter.

She was the woman who "sold purple" and a "worshipper of God"—two distinct descriptions of her. In other words, she was a merchant, and God recognized her as someone who had a heart for him.

Her story reminds the modern woman that having a business or career or profession does not preclude being a woman of God or a woman who has a heart for him.

Further, in this extensive chapter 6, we talked about Lydia's deference to the leaders in God that had preached to her:

> *If in your opinion, I am one really convinced*
> *[that Jesus is the Messiah and the Author of salva-*
> *tion] and that I will be faithful to the Lord, come to*
> *my house and stay. (Acts 16:15 AMPC)*

It was a quality that seems to speak to the totality of a heart. A submissive woman does not particularly mean that the lady is someone who has her head bowed all day long, keeping quiet in a corner and letting the men perform all the leadership tasks.

A submissive woman is synonymous with a humble one. She considers others' opinions, especially those in the household of faith, and who have testimonies of God's supernatural presence in their lives to be higher than hers.

The summary of chapter 6 was an extensive walkthrough with the features of women in the Bible, and the elements about them that could have caused God to notice them so that he was the one who made the effort to have worthy mentions of them in his Word as opposed to their seeking to be mentioned through their own efforts.

In chapter 7, the topic was the Gifts of the Spirit, with the view that these gifts cannot work as intended when there is disunity in the church.

After all, if God is the God of peace, how could he bless or be present in a ministry where there are quarrels about who gets what position, especially if he was not the one handing out those positions by divine appointment so that they are merely human-made in the church?

Examples of individuals that God divinely appointed were mentioned: Moses, Gideon, and David. There was a suggestion during this section that the individuals were pursued by God so that he could bestow positions on them. In other words, he had to convince them! It appears that this is the characteristic of ministries that are God-ordained. The people in those offices were never seeking the opportunity.

It may recommend that those who are not seeking positions have the right hearts that God desires for his posts.

Next, there was chapter 8, which was a conversation about ministry, and, specifically, women in the Old Testament who had it—Dorcas, the woman who did "good works," the daughters of Philip the evangelist who could prophesy, Priscilla and Aquila (always mentioned together) who had a home church and were said to "risk their lives for Paul," and, finally, Phoebe the "helper" to many because she did not like to see people suffering.

An attempt was made to provide some insight into what these women's ministries must have looked like.

In that chapter, the three areas of thought about what a woman's ministry should look like were in prayers, giving, and soul winning. Considering that there were many instances of the sick needing healing and disciples getting arrested in the New Testament, these women must have been heavily involved in prayers.

Also, the environment of the church in the earlier days of its inception was a community where everyone contributed to the same "pot" and distributed those donations according to the individual needs of the church members. Thus, these women must have been givers—a character which the Bible indicates that God loves, if it is cheerfully done.

> *For God loves (He takes pleasure in, prizes above other things, and is unwilling to abandon or to do without) a cheerful (joyous, "prompt to do it") giver [whose heart is in his giving]. (2 Corinthians 9:7)*

As a result, it is very likely that these women's ministries involved a lot of giving since the needs of the entire community depended on it.

Finally, the matter of soul winning was a major one in the early church. It was the platform through which people were informed about the salvation message, the "incredible" notion that God had come to Earth because he is *that* concerned about the human state so that he could experience life as a man and pay a price through sacrifice for the degenerate existence that the world was living.

This area of ministry is not as often emphasized in today's churches it seems, yet it is the core of why Jesus came to the Earth to give his life for mankind.

The purpose of chapter 8 was to provide these ideas of what a woman's ministry would have looked like in the days of the early church—and possibly how it should look like today.

Any woman engaged in these three things—prayer, giving, and soul winning—already has a ministry.

This summarizes what has been discussed so far in the prevalent conversation about why women should have a place in ministry.

Yet there seems to be a showstopper against women to all the aforementioned discourse!

There was an exhortation that Apostle Paul gave to the church in the book of 1 Timothy that would *contradict* the position of everything that was just discussed in this book—the position that God does not exclude women from ministry. Apostle Paul exhorted:

> *Let a woman learn in silence with all submission. And I do not permit a woman to teach or to have authority over a man, but to be in silence. (1 Timothy 2:11–12)*

It would appear that Apostle Paul is contradicting the testimonies of the Old Testament and New Testament. What about Rebecca, who became a guardian for her children's destinies, and spoke with Isaac about how to preserve Jacob's? Deborah, who spoke as a judge for Israel? Or Esther, who presented herself before the king and advocated for the lives of all Jews? Is Apostle Paul saying they should have been "silent" with no ministries?

When considering the commentaries of the premier leaders of the ministries about women and silence in church, it is important to take matters into context.

It is not a stretch of the imagination that many females—and no disrespect is intended—love to speak often. In fact, they may even like to speak a lot. In the church, such a practice would have been unruly. It would contradict the place of God where he had indicated that he wants things to be done in good order.

> *Now I say this for your own welfare and profit, not to put [a halter of] restraint upon you, but to promote what is seemly and in good order. (1 Corinthians 7:35)*

It may be the only and main reason why Apostle Paul would have recommended that females should be "submissive."

A discussion about what *submissive* may mean was mentioned when reviewing the life of Lydia, the woman who sold purple and who God gave a heart that could receive his word without offense. She was humble. She asked about what the Apostles thought regarding her faith. She did not assume that she had "arrived" or that she had a certain quality that made her "a good Christian woman." She requested the views of others who knew better than her.

Submissiveness then is humility. This does not seem a bad ask to make to women in the church. Consider the benefits that the Lord has indicated would be bestowed on a humble individual.

If that was what Apostle Paul was saying, submissiveness equals humility, is he not requesting a good thing from women?

Humility prevents destruction because it is the opposite of pride:

> *When the Lord saw that they humbled themselves, the word of the Lord came to Shemaiah, saying, They have humbled themselves, so I will not destroy them. (2 Chronicles 12:7 AMPC)*

Humility gives honor:

> *A man's pride will bring him low, but he who is of a humble spirit will obtain honor. (Proverbs 29:23 AMPC)*

God "builds up" a humble person.

> *If you return to the Almighty [and submit and humble yourself before Him], you will be built up. (Job 22:23 AMPC)*

He listens to their problems and does not forget.

*He does not forget the cry of the afflicted (the*
*poor and the humble). (Psalm 9:2 AMPC)*

The pages of this book could continue extensively to demonstrate examples of what God provides to those who are submissive—that is, the individual who is humble.

He protects the humble from destruction. For instance, in a world where drugs, violence, and all manner of atrocities exist, God's protection is a very needed commodity.

He grants honor to the humble. What is honor?

It means high respect and esteem. A submissive person receives, by default, respect as opposed to attempting to force it from others or from God.

The building up of God, another benefit he grants to the humble, is multi-faceted: financial, social, spiritual, and any other area where one needs it.

Considering that God controls every aspect of existence, he has a say in every area of life. A humble person gains the access to his solidifying every aspect of their lives with good things.

His ear is open to listen to the cries of the humble. It is a food for thought anytime a believer wonders why God is not responding to cries for help. Perhaps some self-reflection may be needed. Of course, there are situations where help comes later than other instances. Yet when God does not help a person at all, it may be due to a humility issue.

One can conclude then that Apostle Paul, in his "contradictory statement" that women should be submissive or quiet or to not teach in the church, is actually bestowing a blessing on them.

In the eyes of God, they become better candidates for the benefits he gives to the humble.

*But why no teaching?*

Apostle Paul admonished that women should not teach in the church.

While it is stated that his exhortation is helping the women of the church to be humble, is the point he made about "no teaching" really necessary? Being quiet and submissive in order to practice humility is different from being disallowed from teaching!

What did the Apostle mean?

In the days of old Jewish custom, it may be necessary to note that women were not traditionally raised in the knowledge of the Torah, the Jewish Bible. In fact, the Jewish culture was considered to be a very male-dominant one.

While Apostle Paul was respecting the rule of the day—like Jesus said, give to Caesar what belongs to Caesar (government, secular leaders), and to God, what belongs to God—he was also trying to keep order in the church.

Christianity was a new wave in the first century—a wave where God did not discriminate between males and females, an era where women could now start expressing their views and prophesying and talking to people about salvation in God. It was very countercultural. It was a liberation that may have been intoxicating. It could possibly have led to movements of "more female power."

While there is nothing wrong with seeking more opportunities for females in society, the goal of an early church that was trying to establish the rule of God on Earth was not focused on male or female movements.

It was focused on order and getting the job done for the Lord.

For this reason, Apostle Paul's statement may have been much needed. It should not be viewed as censorship of women in the church, but rather, as an opportunity for the church itself to be *disciplined*.

There is one statement that seems similar to this particular point of submissiveness which the Apostle made concerning women's submission in the church.

This other statement will be considered in the next chapter.

# CHAPTER 10
## *Prohibitions*

*Let your women keep silent in the churches, for they are not permitted
to speak; but they are to be submissive, as the law also says. And
if they want to learn something, let them ask their own husbands
at home; for it is shameful for women to speak in church.*

—1 Corinthians 14:34–35

### *Husbands, wives, and church*

The reason why the above scriptural quote warrants a chapter to
itself is because it talks about the very huge topic of marriage.

In the previous chapter, Apostle Paul's statement about women
keeping silent in the church would appear to be so much more innoc-
uous when compared with this other statement that is in review in
this chapter.

He said: Women should "ask their husbands at home." It is a
recommendation that would raise the ire of the most sensitive of
liberal movements.

The passage appears to be asking women to not only be silent
in church, but to defer to their husbands for any opinion they may
try to present around church matters. In fact, they should not only
defer to their husbands for such opinions. They need to defer to him
in *private*. In other words, they should not be found in a public place,
discussing matters of the church with their husbands because it may
suggest that they are being non-submissive.

This statement appears to be giving all power to men in the church.

Before dissecting this thought, it may be beneficial to consider what God thinks about marriage.

> *Husbands, love your wives, as Christ loved the church and gave Himself up for her. (Ephesians 5:25)*

God compares marriage between a man and a woman to the union between Christ and the church.

If Christ is the bridegroom, the church is the bride.

If the church is the bride, she probably would benefit from being submissive to the bridegroom.

After all, it is written:

> *Let the wife see that she respects and reverences her husband [that she notices him, regards him, honors him, prefers him, venerates, and esteems him; and that she defers to him, praises him, and loves and admires him exceedingly]. (Ephesians 5:33 AMPC)*

The picture that 1 Corinthians 14 is trying to provide to the church, or to women, may be that they should submit toward their husbands the way that God expects the church, his bride, to submit toward him.

It is probably true that there are many views of what submission to God means. However, it would probably be surprising if there was a true believer who recommended that submission to God excludes: *"notices him, regards him, honors him, prefers him, venerates, and esteems him; defers to him, praises him, and loves and admires him exceedingly."*

This is exactly how Ephesians 5:33 asks women to behave toward their husbands. It is exactly what God would expect from the church toward him.

Thus, the opening scripture in this chapter is recommending to women that they practice characters that attract God like a man would be attracted to his bride.

Why is this recommendation not being made to men since they are part of the church, too, the bride of Christ?

The reality is that it is made for men. In fact, the exhortation to men is *longer* with regard to how they are to behave around their wives:

> *Husbands, love your wives, as Christ loved the church and gave Himself up for her,*
>
> *So that He might sanctify her, having cleansed her by the washing of water with the Word,*
>
> *That He might present the church to Himself in glorious splendor, without spot or wrinkle or any such things [that she might be holy and faultless].*
>
> *Even so husbands should love their wives as [being in a sense] their own bodies. He who loves his own wife loves himself.*
>
> *For no man ever hated his own flesh, but nourishes and carefully protects and cherishes it, as Christ does the church,*
>
> *Because we are members (parts) of His body.*
>
> *For this reason, a man shall leave his father and his mother and shall be joined to his wife, and the two shall become one flesh.*
>
> *This mystery is very great, but I speak concerning [the relation of] Christ and the church.*
>
> *However, let each man of you [without exception] love his wife as [being in a sense] his very own self. (Ephesians 5:25–33)*

The reader may see the point. The man has his own duties to fulfill as part of the union, both toward the church and toward his wife.

Chapter 9 focused on women keeping silent in the church. This chapter has its focus on women being submissive to their husbands as members of the church.

The final resolution is that these views are not to censure women or belittle them before men.

These ideas are intended to bless them with a different mindset that God approves.

This concludes then that women in ministry are not prohibited. The exhortations about their silence in church or submission to their husbands would, in actuality, give them even better preparedness for any ministry that the Lord may desire to enroll them into.

## Final thoughts

A woman has a place in ministry in the church.

She is a member of the body of God that has been placed in high esteem from the beginning of time. Without her, the world cannot be "fruitful and multiply," from the beginning, in Genesis.

> *Be fruitful, multiply, and fill the earth.*
> *(Genesis 1:28)*

If the reader of this book is female and seeking a ministry in God, she should know that she is qualified from the beginning simply by getting involved in the small community engagements around her.

A woman who has a ministry in her destiny will discover it if she is able to seek God for it or waits on his appointment while she goes about her life, praying, giving, and winning souls for Christ.

A woman is not excluded from the events that have made, and will continue to make, the church succeed.

She has held roles throughout the history of mankind that would suggest that without those roles, certain successes that have occurred in today's world would not have stood a chance. For instance, Jacob, the father of Israel, would likely not have made his destiny if he had not received a great blessing from his father. His mother, Rebecca, orchestrated his receiving it.

Israel may have been defeated by their enemies if any of the judges that God placed within the nation over their years of history had not been available. This means that a woman like Deborah affected their success as a nation.

And of course, Christ could not have been born without a woman.

The *end.*

# REFERENCES

*The Holy Bible: The Amplified Bible.* La Habra, CA: The Lockman
Foundation. Retrieved from https://www.biblegateway.com.

Segal, E. (n.d.). "Vashti, A Feminist Heroine?" Retrieved from http://
people.ucalgary.ca/~elsegal/Shokel/910301_Vashti.html.

Szterszky, S. (n.d.). "Women in the Book of Acts: Real, Diverse and
Essential." Retrieved from https://www.focusonthefamily.ca/
content/women-in-the-book-of-acts-real-diverse-and-essential.

"Women in Ancient Israel." (n.d.). Retrieved from https://www.
bible-history.com/court-of-women/women.html.

# ABOUT THE AUTHOR

Rev. Dr. A. Louise Bonaparte is blessed to be a seventh-generation ordained minister and has been in the ministry for over thirty years. She is an apostle and archbishop in the Lord's church. Clergy and churches in two hundred countries serve under her leadership.

She is also an interfaith minister as well as an ordained reformed rabbi, serving as chairwoman of the board of a prestigious International Board of Rabbis, being the only female and person of color. She is not only anointed but also educated, having earned twelve degrees, of which seven are doctorates. She is currently pursuing another degree and is a doctoral candidate for an EdD in leadership.

Her career spans from Wall Street as a financial adviser to nursing. She has also accomplished becoming a surgical oncologist and scientific researcher.

She is the CEO of her family's ninety-one-year-old enterprise, with employees on every continent. She also is the founder and president of seven nonprofit organizations.

She has received numerous awards and citations (too many to mention) from around the globe.

As a third-generation multimillionaire, she is a guru in teaching generational wealth. She travels the world, teaching various topics to help mankind.